Air on the Move

Peter Mellett
Jane Rossiter

FRANKLIN WATTS

New York • London • Toronto • Sydney

© Franklin Watts 1992

Franklin Watts, Inc.
95 Madison Avenue
New York, NY 10016

Senior editor: Hazel Poole
Series editor: Jane Walker
Designer: Ann Samuel
Illustrator: Annabel Milne
Photographer: Michael Stannard
Consultant: Margaret Whalley

Library of Congress Cataloguing-in-Publication Data

Mellett, P. (Peter), 1946-
    Air on the move / Peter Mellett, Jane Rossiter.
        p.   cm — (Science through cookery)
    Summary: Explains the scientific principles of air and the
different gases it contains. Presents recipes to illustrate these
principles.
    ISBN 0-531-14244-2
    1. Cookery—Juvenile literature.   2. Air—Juvenile literature.
[1. Air.   2. Air—Experiments.   3. Experiments.   4. Cookery.]
I. Rossiter, Jane.   II. Title.   III. Series.
TX652.5.M358 1992
533'.6'078—dc20   92-14719
                                                   CIP   AC

The publisher would like to thank the following
children for their participation in the photography of
this book: Tom Brownrigg, Tom Holloway, Ana Samuel
and Corinne Smith-Williams.

Typeset by Spectrum, London
Printed in Singapore

Contents

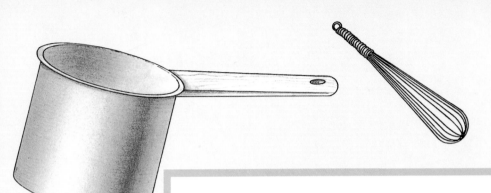

Introduction

Science Through Cookery is a new, simple and fun approach to learning about science. In each book you will not only read about science, but you will also have firsthand experience of real science. By linking science topics with simple cookery recipes, you can learn about science and at the same time create some delicious recipes. Science is fun when you finish up eating the results of your work!

About this book

Air on the Move investigates air, and the different gases that it contains, such as oxygen and carbon dioxide. You can find out why hot air behaves differently from cold air, and discover which gases are heavier or lighter than air. This book also

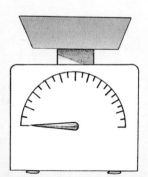

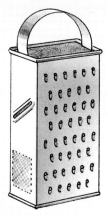

helps you to understand difficult terms, such as air pressure and humidity.

Air on the Move explains important scientific principles with the help of clearly labeled diagrams and illustrations. The recipes offer a practical opportunity to gain a better understanding of the science you have just read about.

Each recipe has been carefully selected and written so that the cooking can be done with a minimum amount of adult supervision. Where the help of an adult is needed, for example when boiling a pot of water, this is clearly indicated.

The ingredients and equipment you will need are listed at the beginning of each recipe. The step-by-step format of the recipes is easy to follow. Each step is illustrated with a photograph.

At the end of the book you will find a page of Further things to do. These are fun experiments and activities which are linked to many of the science concepts discussed in the book. A glossary of terms and an index are provided at the end of the book.

What is a gas?

When you bake a cake or boil some cabbage, a smell soon fills the whole kitchen. Smells are caused by gases, and all gases spread out to fill completely the space they are in.

Solids keep their shape and stay where you put them. Liquids are runny and stay in the bottom of their container. Gases have no definite shape. They escape from their container unless it is closed tightly.

Solids, liquids, and gases are all made up from tiny particles called atoms. The atoms in most substances are joined together in separate groups, called molecules. When a substance is heated, the molecules inside it move around more quickly.

When food is cooking, some of the molecules in the liquid part of the food move so fast that they escape completely as a gas. This change from a liquid to a gas is called evaporation. As a result, the kitchen fills with smells and steam. The steam forms when liquid water changes into a gas.

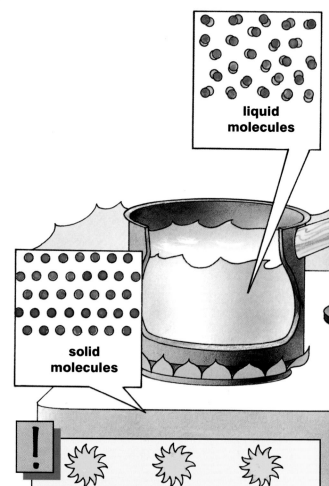

liquid molecules

solid molecules

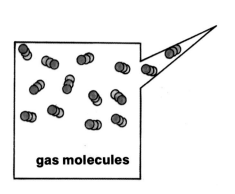

gas molecules

! Some countries are extremely hot and have very little rain. There is not enough fresh water for drinking and cooking. In Saudi Arabia, sea water is used to make about 1,700 million quarts of fresh water each day.

Burning oil or gas boils the seawater, which gives off steam. The steam is piped away while the sea salt stays behind in the boiling liquid. When the steam is cooled, it changes into pure water. This process is called desalination.

Pasta shapes in tomato sauce

Ingredients

1 onion
2 cloves garlic
2 16oz cans of
   chopped tomatoes
1 tablespoon oil
2 teaspoons dried basil
1 teaspoon dried thyme
1 tablespoon
   tomato puree
3¼oz water
salt and pepper
8oz pasta shapes

Equipment

a cutting board
a knife
a can opener
2 saucepans
a wooden spoon
a teaspoon
a tablespoon
a measuring cup
a colander
a serving dish

1 Peel the onion, then chop it into small pieces. Peel the cloves of garlic and chop them into very small pieces.

2 Measure the oil into a saucepan and add the onion and garlic. Stir, then cook over a medium-low heat for 5 minutes. Turn the heat down if they begin to brown.

3 Carefully open the cans of tomatoes and add them to the saucepan. Add the herbs, tomato puree, salt, pepper, and water. Stir well, turn up the heat, and bring the mixture to the boil.

4 When the mixture is boiling, lower the heat so that the sauce simmers gently. Put on the lid and cook for 20 minutes.

5 Half-fill the second saucepan with water. Ask an adult to help you bring it to a boil, then carefully add the pasta shapes. Boil the pasta, without a lid, for 10–12 minutes.

6 Remove the lid from the sauce after 20 minutes. Stir well and continue to simmer, without the lid, for another 20 minutes until the sauce has thickened.

7 When the pasta is cooked, ask an adult to help you drain it through the colander placed in the bottom of the sink. Arrange the pasta on a serving dish and pour the sauce over it.

The air

Air is all around us. It is a mixture of many different gases. The main ones are oxygen and nitrogen. About one-fifth of the air is oxygen. We breathe oxygen, which helps to release energy from our food. Fuels like coal, oil, and natural gas need oxygen to burn.

Nitrogen gas makes up about four-fifths of the air. Factories use nitrogen to make fertilizers that help food crops to grow. Tiny creatures called bacteria, which live in the soil, also use nitrogen to help plants to grow. Less than 1 percent of air is argon, which is a colorless, odorless gas. The argon used inside light bulbs keeps the wire filament from burning away.

Air also contains very small amounts of carbon dioxide. This gas is given out when animals breathe and fuels burn. Plants take in carbon dioxide from the air to make their own food and to grow. At the same time, they give out oxygen.

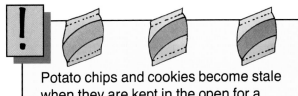

Potato chips and cookies become stale when they are kept in the open for a long time. They contain fats that are altered by the oxygen in the air. The fats start to have a bad odor and become unpleasant to eat. Potato chips and cookies are sold in sealed packages that contain oxygen-free air. Without oxygen, the food stays fresh much longer.

All plants need carbon dioxide gas to grow. Tomatoes in greenhouses grow faster when extra carbon dioxide is added to the air.

This pie chart shows the mixture and amount of the different gases that make up the air.

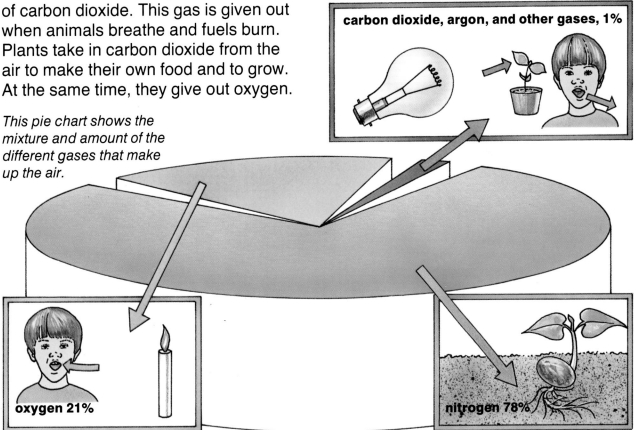

carbon dioxide, argon, and other gases, 1%

oxygen 21%

nitrogen 78%

Oxygen and carbon dioxide

About one-fifth of the air is oxygen. Like other animals, we breathe in air and use the oxygen in it to release energy from our food. This energy helps us to move and to grow. The air we breathe out contains carbon dioxide. Making energy and carbon dioxide from food and oxygen is called respiration.

The amount of oxygen and carbon dioxide in the air around us stays about the same. As we use up oxygen and give out carbon dioxide, plants are doing exactly the opposite. They take in carbon dioxide through their leaves, and water through their roots. They use energy from sunlight to join these substances together to make their own foods, like sugar and starch. At the same time, they give out oxygen. This process is called photosynthesis. Respiration and photosynthesis keep carbon dioxide on the move.

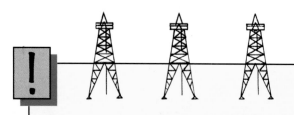

Coal, oil, and natural gas are fossil fuels. They are the remains of plants and tiny animals that lived on Earth millions of years ago. When we burn these fossil fuels, we use up oxygen and make carbon dioxide. There are not enough plants living now to use up all the carbon dioxide we produce in this way.

The amount of carbon dioxide in the air is slowly increasing. It is trapping the heat from the sun, and making the world become warmer. Scientists call this "the greenhouse effect," and they think it may alter the world's weather.

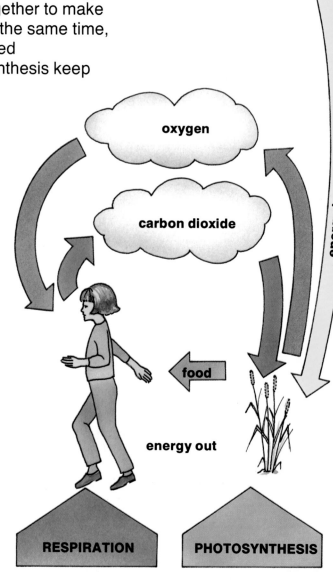

oxygen

carbon dioxide

energy in

food

energy out

RESPIRATION

PHOTOSYNTHESIS

Fruit syrup

Ingredients
2lbs berry fruits, such as
  blackberries, blackcurrants,
  raspberries, and redcurrants
2 cups superfine sugar

Equipment

2 large bowls
a potato masher
a dish towel
a jelly bag
food scale

a tablespoon
a large measuring cup
  (1-quart size)
a clean bottle with
  a screw-top lid

1 First wash then place the fruit in a large bowl and squash it with the potato masher until it is juicy. Cover the bowl with the dish towel and keep in a warm place for 24 hours.

2 The fruit will now have bubbles of carbon dioxide gas on the surface. Ask a friend to hold the jelly bag over the second bowl, and carefully pour the fruit into the bag. Hang the bag up above the bowl and let the juice drip overnight.

3 The next day, squeeze the bag to get out as much juice as possible. Throw away the pulp in the bag, and pour the juice into the measuring cup. Add 2 cups of sugar for every 2 cups of juice. Stir until the sugar has dissolved.

4 Pour the syrup into the clean bottle and screw on the lid. Keep the syrup in the refrigerator. Serve with ice cream, or add water to make a fruit drink.

Rising air

The air is hot above the candles on a birthday cake. Heat travels up from the tiny flames. Why does hot air rise upward?

The cold air around the flames becomes hotter. When air is heated, it expands and takes up more space. We say that hot air is less dense than cold air. This means that a balloon full of hot air weighs less than a balloon of the same size that is full of cold air.

Do you know what happens when cooking oil is shaken up in a jar with water? When you put down the jar, the mixture slowly separates. The oil, which is less dense, floats upward, but the water, which is more dense, sinks downward. In the same way, hot air rises from the candles because it is less dense than the cold air around it.

The hot air cools as it rises from the candles. As it cools, it becomes more dense and eventually starts to sink. This movement of air is called a convection current.

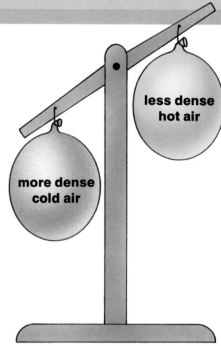

These balloons are hanging from a beam scale. The air in the top balloon is hot. The air in the bottom balloon is cold.

convection current

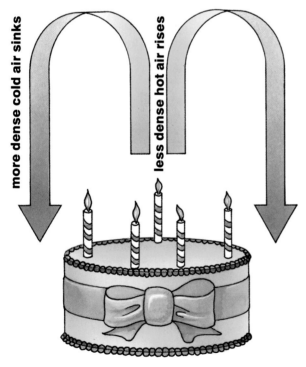

more dense cold air sinks

less dense hot air rises

The burner inside a gas oven is fitted at the bottom, but the freezer inside a refrigerator is fitted at the top. Convection currents carry heat upward inside an oven. The hot air cooks food on the shelves above. At the same time, cooler air sinks toward the burner.

In a refrigerator, convection currents carry cold air downward from the freezer. The cold air cools food on the shelves below. At the same time, warmer air rises upward toward the freezer.

Lemon cakes

Ingredients
1 lemon
3½ oz softened margarine
3½ oz superfine sugar
2 eggs
3½ oz self-rising flour

Equipment
food scale
a grater
a plate
a large bowl
a wooden spoon
a measuring cup
a fork
a sifter
a tablespoon
a teaspoon
12 paper baking cups
a muffin tin or cookie
  sheet
a wire cooling rack

1 Grate the yellow rind of the lemon on a fine grater. Set the oven to 350°F. Measure or weigh out the margarine and sugar and put them in the bowl.

2 Cream the margarine and sugar by beating them together with the wooden spoon. The creamed mixture should be pale in color, light and fluffy.

3 Break the eggs into the cup and beat them with the fork. Add the eggs, a little at a time, to the sugar mixture and beat well each time with the wooden spoon.

4 Place the sifter over the bowl and add the flour. Shake the sifter so that the flour goes into the bowl. Add the lemon rind.

5 Use the tablespoon to stir the flour and lemon rind into the mixture as gently as possible.

6 Arrange the paper baking cups in the muffin tin or on the cookie sheet. Use the teaspoon to add the mixture to the cups. Put the tin or cookie sheet in the oven.

7 Bake the cakes for about 10 minutes until they are golden and well risen. Carefully remove from the oven, using oven mitts, and transfer them to the wire rack to cool.

Hot and cold air

Puff pastry swells up and becomes light and crispy when it is baked. This happens because the pastry is rolled and folded over many times before it is placed in the oven. When the pastry is folded, air is trapped between the layers of pastry. During cooking, this air is heated and makes the pastry swell.

Like all gases, air is made up from atoms and molecules. These atoms and molecules are moving about all the time. When the air inside the puff pastry is heated, the molecules move around faster. The air now takes up more space and pushes apart the layers of pastry.

When a handful of corn is heated up in very hot oil, its size increases more than 20 times to make popcorn. Why does popcorn pop?

Corn is very hard and contains tiny bubbles of trapped air. When the corn is heated, the trapped air tries to expand. The molecules of air speed around and push with more and more force against the hard walls of the tiny bubbles. Suddenly the bubbles burst, and the grains of corn explode into light and fluffy popcorn.

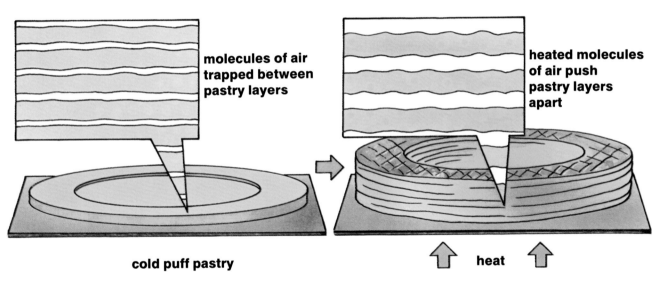

molecules of air trapped between pastry layers

heated molecules of air push pastry layers apart

cold puff pastry

heat

When gases are heated, they expand and take up more space. The amount of a gas is measured by its volume, which tells you how much space the gas takes up. Volume is measured in units called gallons, and 1 gallon is equal to 128 fluid ounces. When a gas heats up, its volume increases. When a gas cools, it contracts and takes up less space, so its volume becomes less.

The volume of lemonade in this bottle is 1 quart, or 2 pints.

Apple turnovers

Ingredients
2 large cooking apples
1 tablespoon water
1 tablespoon sugar
¼ teaspoon ground cinnamon
3½oz plain flour
1oz white fat *
1¾oz butter or stick margarine *
a pinch of salt
1 teaspoon lemon juice
3oz cold water
extra flour for rolling
a little sugar

* cold from the refrigerator

Equipment
a cutting board
a knife
a tablespoon
a teaspoon
a 1½ qt pot with a lid
a wooden spoon
food scale
a sifter
a large bowl
a measuring cup
a palette knife
a rolling pin
a pastry brush
a cookie sheet

1 Peel, core, and slice the apples. Put them in the pot with the water, sugar, and cinnamon. Put on the lid and cook, over a low heat, for 10–15 minutes until the apples are soft. Remove from the heat and mix with the wooden spoon. Leave to cool.

2 Sift the flour and salt into the bowl. Add the fat and rub it into the flour between your thumbs and fingers until the fat disappears.

3 Cut the butter or margarine into small squares. Add the butter, lemon juice, and most of the water to the bowl. Mix with the palette knife.

4 Press the mixture together to form a lumpy dough. Use the rest of the water if needed. Turn out the dough onto a floured surface.

5 Use the palette knife and rolling pin to shape the dough into a block. Roll the dough evenly into an oblong shape, about $\frac{1}{8}$ inch thick. Use the palette knife to keep the edges straight and the corners square.

6 Fold down the top third of the pastry. Fold up the bottom third and press the edges together with the rolling pin. Turn the pastry a quarter turn, so the fold is on your left.

7 Roll the pastry into an oblong shape and fold and turn again. Repeat four times in all. Use extra flour if the dough is sticky. Preheat the oven to 350°F.

8 Roll the pastry into a thin square and divide it into 4 small squares. Spoon the cooled apple onto the diagonal half of each square, leaving a ½-inch gap around the edge.

9 Dampen the pastry edges with water. Fold each square into a triangle, and seal the edges with your thumb. Put the turnovers on the sheet.

10 Brush the turnovers with a little water and sprinkle with sugar. Bake for 25–30 minutes until the pastry is puffed and brown.

Lighter or heavier than air?

Smoke rises from the toaster when you burn a slice of toast. The smoke is made from tiny particles that are carried upward by a stream of hot air. This stream of hot air is called a convection current. Hot air rises because it is less dense than the cold air around it.

Party balloons that float up to the ceiling are filled with a gas called helium. This gas is about eight times less dense than air. Carbon dioxide, which is given off by substances such as yeast and baking powder, is more dense than air. So you would not fill a party balloon with carbon dioxide.

Yeast helps to make wine and beer. The carbon dioxide gas that is given off by the yeast is collected from breweries. It is used to fill certain kinds of fire extinguisher.

When carbon dioxide is released around a fire, it forms a dense and heavy layer that sinks onto the flames and keeps the air away. Fire cannot burn without the oxygen in air, and so the flames die down.

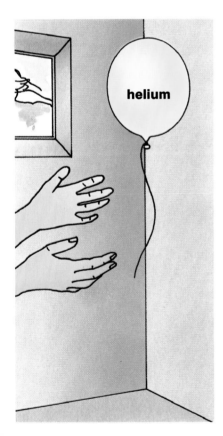

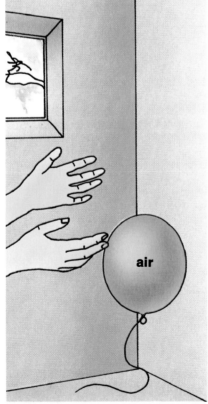

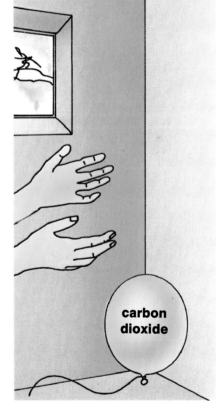

Helium is less dense than air, and so the balloon floats upward.

The air inside the balloon has the same density as the air in the room.

Carbon dioxide is more dense than air, and so the balloon sinks.

Sweet corn fritters

Ingredients
6 oz plain flour
½ teaspoon baking powder
1 egg
5 oz milk
10½ oz sweet corn
salt and pepper
oil for frying

Equipment
food scale
a sifter
a bowl
a measuring cup
a wooden spoon
a tablespoon
a frying pan (8–10 inch)
a spatula

1 Sift the flour and the baking powder into the bowl. Make a well in the middle. Break the egg into the well, and add half the milk.

2 Use the wooden spoon to mix the egg and milk into the flour. Beat the mixture well to get rid of any lumps, then gradually add the rest of the milk.

3 Add the sweet corn to the flour mixture. Season with salt and pepper and mix together thoroughly. Ask an adult to help you heat a little oil in the frying pan.

4 Add the mixture, one tablespoon at a time, to the pan. You can fit about four fritters in the pan. Fry until firm and brown underneath, then turn the fritter over and cook the other side. Serve at once.

Water in the air

When you boil pots of water, the air in the kitchen feels hot and steamy. Droplets of water start to trickle down the cold windowpanes. The heat from the stove gives energy to the molecules of water in the pots. This energy makes the molecules move about faster. Water molecules are quite small and light, and they start to move so fast that some escape. Heat makes liquid water evaporate and become water vapor.

The amount of water vapor in the air is called the humidity. The humidity of warm air can be greater than the humidity of cold air. You cannot see the water vapor in the air, but you can see its effects. Warm and humid air cools when it meets a cold window. The molecules of water vapor slow down and stick together, forming droplets of water that collect on the windowpane.

water vapor cools to form droplets of water

water vapor forms

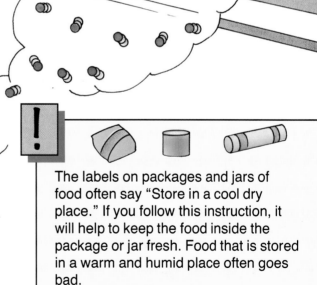

The labels on packages and jars of food often say "Store in a cool dry place." If you follow this instruction, it will help to keep the food inside the package or jar fresh. Food that is stored in a warm and humid place often goes bad.

The air is full of tiny living things called microbes. If these microbes settle on food, they grow and multiply and give out substances that spoil the food. When the air is warm and humid, each microbe splits in half and grows again every 20 minutes.

21

Cheese and broccoli puddings

Ingredients
2oz wholewheat bread (without crusts)
2½oz cheddar cheese
1oz broccoli florets
2oz milk
2 eggs
1 teaspoon mustard
salt and pepper
butter or margarine for greasing

Equipment

a pot, with a steamer
a cutting board
a knife
a cheese grater
a bowl
4 ramekin dishes
a measuring cup
a fork
a wooden spoon
paper towels
aluminum foil
a serving dish

1 Ask an adult to boil a pot of water. Rub the bread on the grater to make crumbs, and put them in the bowl. Grate the cheese and add it to the bowl.

2 Wash the broccoli and cut it into very small pieces. Add the broccoli pieces to the bowl. Mix everything together with your hands.

3 Measure the milk into the cup. Break the eggs into the cup and add the mustard, salt, and pepper. Whisk the ingredients together with the fork.

4 Pour the egg mixture onto the bread crumbs and mix well with the wooden spoon.

5 Use the paper towels and the butter or margarine to grease the insides of each ramekin dish. Divide the mixture between the ramekins, pressing it down gently with the back of the spoon.

6 Cover the ramekins tightly with the foil. Place them in the steamer. Ask an adult to place the steamer over the pot of boiling water. Steam for 30 minutes.

7 Ask an adult to remove the puddings from the steamer. Remove the foil and run the knife around the edge of each dish. Turn the puddings out onto a dish and serve at once.

What is air pressure?

You cannot boil an egg at the top of Mount Everest, the world's highest mountain! When water boils there, the temperature of the water is not hot enough to cook the egg. Eggs usually boil in water at a temperature of 212 degrees Fahrenheit (212°F for short). But 29,028 feet up, at the top of Mount Everest, water boils at about 158°F. Do you know why?

We live at the bottom of an ocean of air. The weight of the air presses down on the outside of everything. The effect of this force is called air pressure. Down at sea level, air pressure is the same as the weight of 10 cars pressing down on every 1.2 square yards of a surface.

Water boils when the water molecules are moving fast enough for bubbles of water vapor to grow. The pressure of the molecules of water vapor as they make a bubble grow must be greater than the pressure of the air trying to make the bubble shrink. The higher up you are, then the lower is the air pressure. The air pressure is so low at the top of Mount Everest that water boils at a lower temperature than it does at sea level. The water is not even hot enough to cook an egg.

Potatoes can take 25 minutes to cook in a pot of water that boils at 212°F. They take about 8 minutes to cook in a pressure cooker.

A pressure cooker is a thick pot with an airtight lid. When water boils in it, the steam is trapped inside. The pressure of the steam pushes down on the water. The water boils at a higher temperature than normal. The temperature inside a pressure cooker is about 240°F.

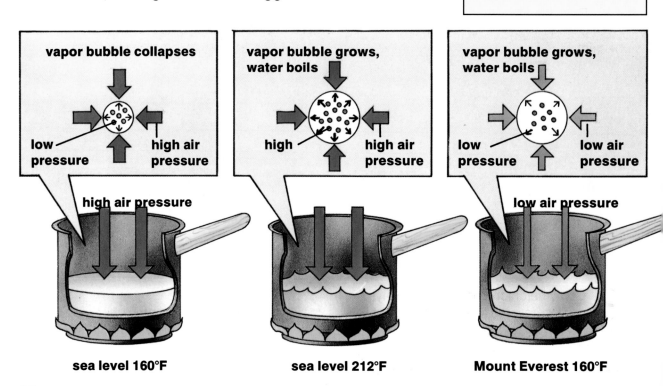

vapor bubble collapses

low pressure   high air pressure

high air pressure

sea level 160°F

vapor bubble grows, water boils

high   high air pressure

sea level 212°F

vapor bubble grows, water boils

low pressure   low air pressure

low air pressure

Mount Everest 160°F

Carrot and lentil soup

Ingredients

1 onion
8oz carrots
1oz butter or margarine
3 teaspoons ground coriander
6oz red lentils
1 teaspoon dried thyme
1 vegetable stock cube
2 cups plus 3oz water

Equipment

a cutting board
a knife
a teaspoon
food scale
a measuring cup
a wooden spoon
a pressure cooker

1 Peel the onion and chop it into small pieces. Peel the carrots and chop them into small pieces.

2 Melt the butter or margarine in the pressure cooker over a medium heat. Add the chopped onion and carrots to the pressure cooker.

3 Cook the onion and carrots slowly, stirring from time to time, for about 5 minutes. Add the coriander to the pan. Cook for a further 2 minutes.

4 Add the thyme and stock cube to the pressure cooker, together with the lentils.

5 Pour in the water and turn up the heat. Put on the lid, and ask an adult to help you bring the soup to a boil.

6 Then, have the adult bring the soup up to high pressure. Cook under pressure for 15 minutes.

7 Ask an adult to show you how to release the pressure. Allow the soup to cool slightly before tasting it. Add salt and pepper if needed, then serve.

Air in food

When you whisk an egg white, it seems to grow larger. The volume of the liquid increases by three or four times because the whisking action traps tiny bubbles of air. If you add sugar to the mixture and bake it in the oven, the result is crispy meringues. Heat makes the bubbles of air expand as the egg white cooks hard.

- Yeast can change a teaspoon of sugar into about 5 quarts of carbon dioxide gas.

- The mass of air in a fairly large kitchen is about 110 pounds – the same as 110 bags of sugar. As much as 1 quart of water can be present in the air as water vapor.

- The ice that builds up in a freezer comes from water vapor in the air. If you melt this ice, the result is pure water.

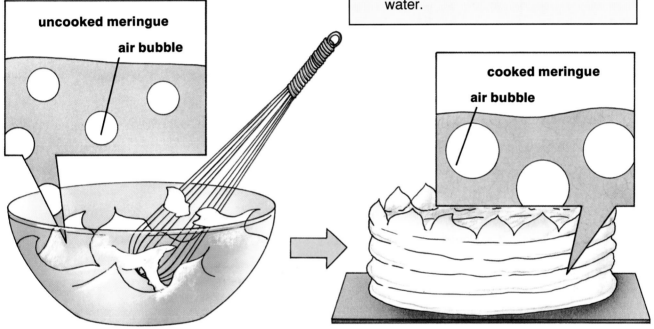

uncooked meringue
air bubble

cooked meringue
air bubble

Small lumps of dough mixture rise as they bake and become large loaves of bread. A slice of bread seems to be full of tiny holes. Why does dough rise, and what makes the holes?

Bakers add yeast to dough, and cooks add baking powder when making cake mixture. Yeast and baking powder both give off bubbles of carbon dioxide gas as the wet ingredients are mixed together. The bubbles are trapped in the mixture and expand, both before and during baking.

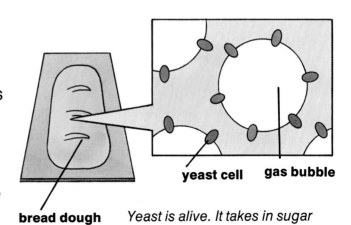

yeast cell   gas bubble

bread dough

Yeast is alive. It takes in sugar and gives out carbon dioxide gas.

Fruity meringue nests

Ingredients

2 eggs
3½oz superfine sugar
8oz heavy cream
fruits, such as strawberries,
    pineapple, raspberries, and
    kiwi fruit

Equipment

a cup and saucer
a small bowl
a large bowl
an electric mixer
a tablespoon
a cookie sheet
baking parchment
a little vegetable oil
a pastry brush
a wire cooling rack

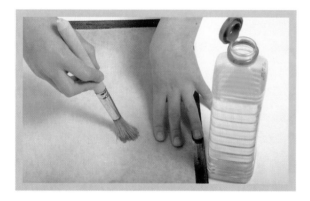

1 Preheat the oven to 200°F. Make sure that all the equipment is very clean and free from grease. Line the cookie sheet with the parchment, and brush on the oil.

2 To separate the egg yolks from the whites, break an egg onto the saucer. Place the upturned cup over the yolk and gently tip the white into the small bowl.

3 Transfer the white to the large bowl and repeat with the second egg. Beat the whites until they are stiff, and no longer slide around when you tilt the bowl.

4 Add half of the sugar and beat again until the whites are very stiff. Add the rest of the sugar. Use the tablespoon to fold in the sugar as gently as possible.

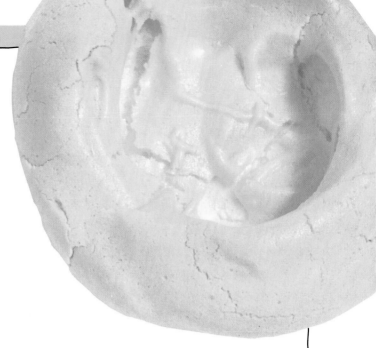

5 Heap 2 tablespoons of the meringue mixture onto the cookie sheet. Flatten it into a circle, and use the back of the spoon to hollow out the middle of the nest.

6 You will be able to make 6–8 nests. Leave about 1½ inches between the nests so they can expand when cooking. Carefully put the cookie sheet in the oven for about 45 minutes to 1 hour.

7 When the nests have risen and are firm, use oven mitts to remove them from the oven. Cool the nests for a few minutes, then transfer onto the wire rack.

8 Pour the heavy cream into the small bowl and beat until stiff. When the nests are cold, put a spoonful of cream into each nest. Top with pieces of fruit.

Further things to do

Put a teaspoon of fresh or dried yeast into a glass jar. Fill the jar one-third full with warm water and add a teaspoon of sugar. Cover the jar with a saucer.

   The mixture will froth up with carbon dioxide in 30 minutes. Ask an adult to lower a lighted match into the jar. It will go out because carbon dioxide does not allow things to burn.

Repeat the previous activity using a bottle with a narrow neck, instead of the glass jar. Tie a balloon around the top of the bottle. The balloon will slowly fill up with the carbon dioxide gas that is given off by the yeast.

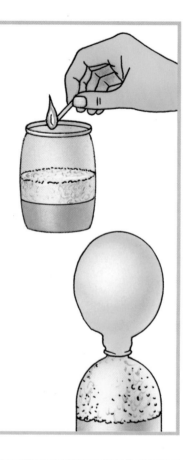

Pour water into a small soda bottle until it is one-quarter full. Make a sausage of thin paper containing two teaspoons of baking powder. Drop the sausage into the bottle and quickly push a cork into the top of the bottle.

   Wet baking powder gives off carbon dioxide gas. The pressure builds up inside the bottle and blows the cork out of the bottle. **Make sure the top of the bottle points away from your face.**

Hold an empty 2-liter plastic bottle upside down with its neck in a bowl of water. Wrap a hot wet cloth around the bottle. The air in the bottle expands as it heats up. You will see air escaping from the bottle and bubbling up through the water.

You can use potato chips to check the humidity of the air. Seal a few chips in a plastic bag. Place paper bags of chips in the bathroom, the kitchen, and the living room. After a day, test the chips in each bag by biting them. Compare each bag of chips with the ones in the plastic bag. The bigger the crunch, the less humid is the air.

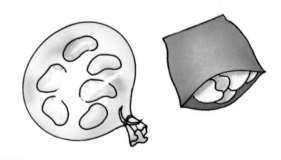

Glossary

argon
A gas that makes up less than 1 percent of the air. It helps to stop things from burning, melting, or changing into other substances.

atom
The smallest part of any substance. There are about 100 different types of atom.

carbon dioxide
A gas that makes up 0.03 percent of the air. It is given out by most living things, but it is taken in by plants.

contract
To become smaller. Gases contract when they are cooled.

convection current
The movement of a stream of gas or liquid that has been heated or cooled.

degree Fahrenheit
A unit that is used to measure temperature. It is written as °F for short.

dense
Describes a substance that is heavier than the same volume of another substance

energy
Energy is the "power" that makes things do work. It can take the form of heat or movement. Energy can be contained in food and in fuels.

evaporate
The way in which a liquid slowly changes into a gas.

expand
To become bigger. Gases expand when they are heated.

fertilizer
A substance that is added to soil to make plants grow well

force
A push that tries to make something move

helium
A gas that is similar to argon, but it is much less dense than air

humid
Describes air that contains a lot of water vapor

mass
A measurement that shows how much matter is in something. Mass is measured in pounds.

molecule
A tiny part that makes up most substances. Each molecule contains two or more atoms.

oxygen
A gas that makes up one-fifth of the air. It is used by animals and by burning fuels. Plants give out oxygen.

nitrogen
A gas that makes up four-fifths of the air. It does not burn.

photosynthesis
The way in which plants use carbon dioxide and energy from the sun to make food and oxygen

pressure
The effect of a force that pushes against a surface

respiration
The way in which animals use food and oxygen to make energy and carbon dioxide

square yard
A measurement of an area that is a square, with each side of the square measuring 1 yard long

temperature
A measurement that shows how hot or cold something is. It is measured in degrees Fahrenheit.

vapor
Another word for gas

volume
A measurement that shows how much space a solid, a liquid, or a gas takes up. Volume is measured in gallons.

weight
The effect of the earth's gravity pulling down on the mass of something gives it weight.

Index